LET'S VISIT URUGUAY

Let's visit
URUGUAY

MARION MORRISON

First published 1985

ACKNOWLEDGEMENTS

The author and publishers are grateful to the following organizations and individuals for permission to reproduce copyright photographs in this book:

CIRIC/Andes Press Agency; The Mansell Collection Limited; Tony and Kimball Morrison/South American Pictures.

CIP data
Morrison, Marion
Let's visit Uruguay
1. Uruguay – Social life and customs – Juvenile Literature
I. Title
989.5'065 F2710

ISBN 0 222 00953 5

Burke Publishing Company Limited
Pegasus House, 116-120 Golden Lane, London EC1Y 0TL, England.
Burke Publishing (Canada) Limited
Registered Office: 20 Queen Street West, Suite 3000, Box 30, Toronto, Canada M5H 1V5.
Burke Publishing Company Inc.
Registered Office: 333 State Street, PO Box 1740, Bridgeport, Connecticut 06601, U.S.A.
Filmset in Baskerville by Graphiti (Hull) Ltd., Hull, England.
Colour reproduction by Swift Graphics (UK) Ltd., Southampton, England.
Printed in Singapore by Tien Wah Press (Pte.) Ltd.

Contents

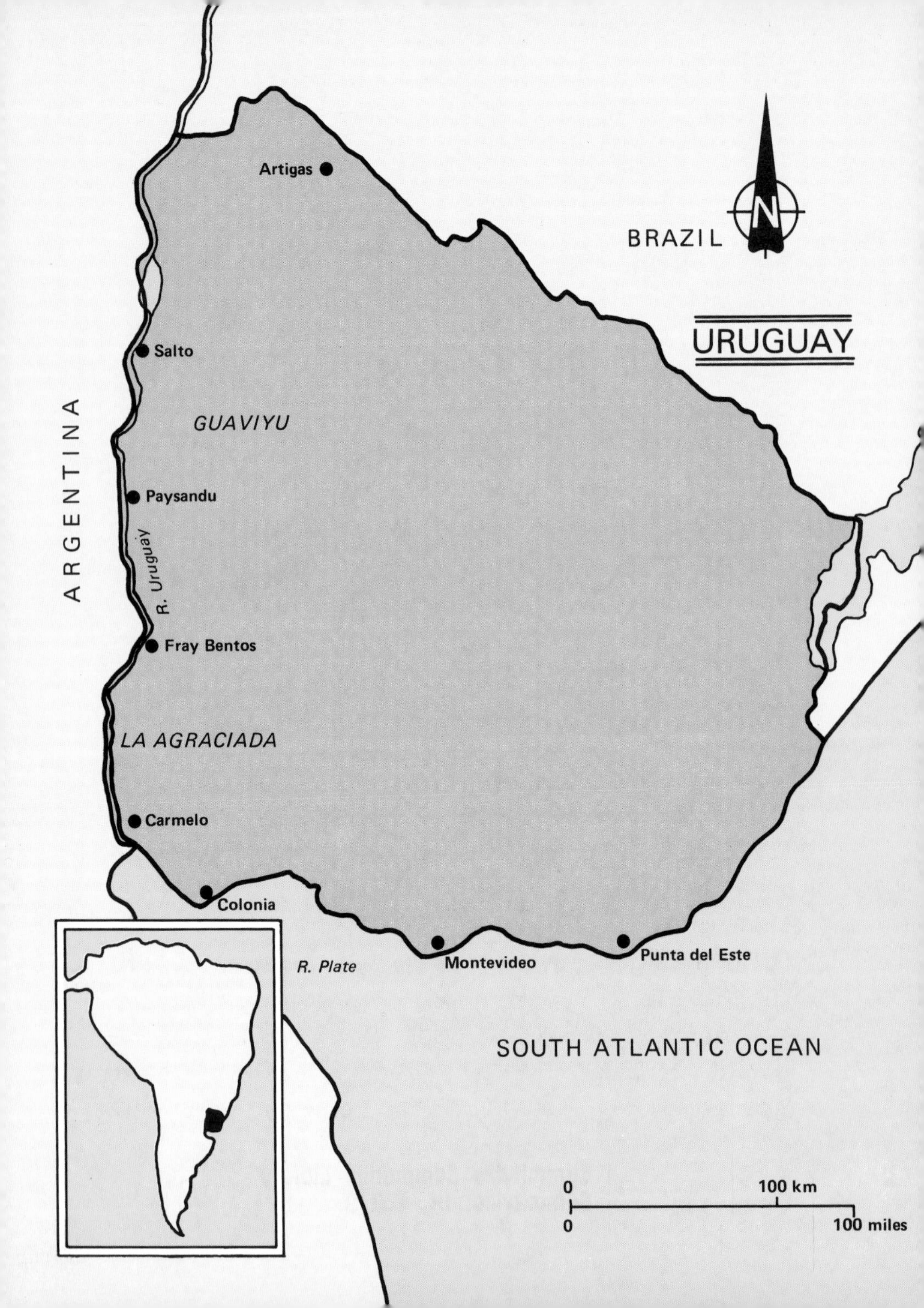
URUGUAY
BRAZIL
N
ARGENTINA
Artigas
Salto
GUAVIYU
Paysandu
R. Uruguay
Fray Bentos
LA AGRACIADA
Carmelo
Colonia
Montevideo
Punta del Este
R. Plate
SOUTH ATLANTIC OCEAN
0
100 km
0
100 miles

The Banda Oriental

Garibaldi, the nineteenth-century Italian freedom fighter spent several years in Uruguay. Long after he had left its shores in 1848, he wrote:

> "Lands, so favoured by nature, inhabited chiefly by horses and cattle, deer and ostriches, where man is a veritable centaur."

For it was in this tiny South American republic that Garibaldi prepared his recruits to fight for the independence of Italy, his native land. The story goes that the famous red shirts worn by the freedom-fighters, were acquired from slaughter-houses in Montevideo, the capital city of Uruguay.

The official title of the country is the Republica Oriental del Uruguay (Eastern Republic of Uruguay), but many local people still call it the *Banda Oriental* (East Bank). This name derives from the country's location on the east bank of the River Uruguay. From early in the sixteenth century until independence in the nineteenth century, the region was part of the Spanish colonial empire in South America. Together with the "west bank" of the River Uruguay, which is now Argentina, it was governed by a Viceroy whose seat was in present-day Buenos Aires. The "east bank" was largely ignored in colonial times. It was not on the route between Buenos Aires and the wealthy gold and silver trails of the Andean countries of Peru and Bolivia, and few people bothered to go there.

The name of the country was probably taken from the name of the river. It is thought to have its origins long ago in the language of the Guarani Indians who once inhabited southern Brazil where the river has its source. The most probable translation is "the river of shellfish" as *urugua* in the Guarani Indian language is the name for a species of mussel.

Uruguay is one of the smallest countries in South America. It might never have become an independent republic but for the determination of its people to free themselves from their two powerful neighbours. Both Brazil and Argentina tried to annexe the tiny territory. Brazil, the largest country in South America, shares Uruguay's border to the north. Argentina is both on the west (separated by the River Uruguay) and to the south (separated from Uruguay by the estuary of the River Plate). To the south-east, Uruguay has an Atlantic coastline, stretching from Brazil south to the mouth of the River Plate. With a total area of only 179,000 square kilometres (72,000 square miles), Uruguay could be compared to a garden plot between two vast estates.

Looking across the River Uruguay—from which the country takes its name—from Salto to Concordia in Argentina

In its unique location, Uruguay is a buffer state, and this is reflected in the physical geography of the country. It is within its territory that the vast open *pampas* (grasslands) of Argentina meet the rolling hills which extend southwards from the Parana Plateau of Brazil. Here, old is meeting young. While the *pampas* are composed of young sediments, the eroded hills are geologically much older. It is a gentle meeting of undulating grassy slopes, broken here and there by weathered, angular granite rock breaking into the skyline, a form known locally as *cuchillas* (crests or ridges). To the west and north, the hills are known as the Cuchilla de Haedo; to the south, where they start near the coastline and extend to the north-east, as the Cuchilla

The *pampas*, or grasslands, of northern Uruguay

Grande. The hills are not high, the tallest peak being the Cerro Catedral at 513 metres (1,700 feet).

Uruguay lacks the remarkable features found in other South American countries. It has no snow-capped mountains, no volcanoes, no tropical jungle, no barren desert and no great forests. At first sight, the countryside is simply green, flat and uniform, with grass extending in every direction as far as the eye can see. It is only on a second meeting that the slopes become obvious—the continuous, never-ending, undulating slopes. There is hardly a tree to break the view. Except for a few bare hilltops and some sandy stretches on the coast, the land is covered by tall prairie grass, said to be superior to that of Argentina, owing to the potash-rich black soil in which it grows. In the broad uplands, sheep and cattle roam and breed. This is the home of horsemen. Their crude huts built from bricks of adobe mud are scattered in remote places that can easily be cut off when rivers and streams flood and make the beaten earth tracks impassable.

There are no major rivers entirely within Uruguay. The Rio Negro, the largest river, rises in southern Brazil and crosses the country from north-east to south-west to flow into the River Uruguay. But many streams flow west from the central hills, down narrow, densely wooded valleys and across flood-plains into the River Plate system, or east to lagoons which lie behind the sandy dune-lined beaches of the Atlantic coast. Still others drain, by way of small estuaries, into the ocean.

Along the Atlantic seaboard, from Uruguay's frontier with

Cattle on a Uruguayan ranch. Meat has long provided the mainstay of the country's economy

Brazil, white sandy beaches extend down the coastline to the estuary of the River Plate. It is a beautiful coastline, over 320 kilometres (200 miles) long, with an endless succession of small bays, beaches and promontories set among hills and woods. A long stretch of the extreme north-east coast is open to a huge lagoon, the Laguna Merim, bounded on the east by a narrow strip of land owned by Brazil and barring the way to the Atlantic. The international boundary follows a line through the centre of the lagoon. A road along the seaward side connects the town of 18 de Julio in Uruguay to Chuy in Brazil.

The most famous headland of the Uruguayan coast is Punta del Este, flanked by large planted forests of eucalyptus, pine and mimosa. To the east of the headland, big salty Atlantic waves roll against the shore. On the west side, the water is calm and brackish. For this reason, Punta del Este is sometimes considered to mark the point where the open ocean meets the brown waters of the River Plate. Here, the coastline turns inland—westwards—and it is on the northern shore of the river that Uruguay's capital, Montevideo, is situated.

Montevideo was founded by the Spaniards in 1726, but the hill behind the city was known to sailors long before then. They used to look out for it at the end of their journeys across the vast oceans. The northern side of the estuary of the River Plate is much deeper than the southern side, so large ships have always been able to approach near to this shore. The port of Montevideo grew in importance and, as it grew, the city developed behind it. Today, Montevideo is the only large town in Uruguay, and

A view of Montevideo, Uruguay's capital city, which is the hub of the country's commercial and political life

it is the hub of the country's commercial and political life.

This southern part of Uruguay has a greater concentration of people than the north. The land here is devoted almost entirely to agriculture. Small-holdings and modest farms dot the landscape, while villages and roadside development feature significantly. None of the towns is large. Minas has 25,000 inhabitants and is involved mostly with servicing the agricultural industry, or producing the mineral water for which the town is famous.

Autumn harrowing on a farm in Uruguay

Inland, between the *cuchillas* where the land is dissected by innumerable small streams or brooks, locally called *arroyos,* the countryside is open. Good roads, linking the towns, are fenced against straying animals. And, while a few trains connect major centres, most Uruguayans use the excellent bus services to reach such towns as Paso de los Toros. This town is favoured by anglers as it is near the extensive artificial lake, called Rincon del Bonete, which has been formed behind the Dr. Gabriel Terra Dam on the Rio Negro.

Along the Brazilian border in the north, towns such as Artigas and Rivera are connected by highways both with Montevideo and with the southern cities of Brazil such as Porto Alegre. International buses travel daily between the two countries.

Seldom is the weather harsh anywhere in Uruguay. The

climate is tempered by the neighbouring Atlantic so that the winters are less cold and the summers less hot than would otherwise be the case. The average temperature for the summer months of January and February is about 22 degrees Celsius (71 degrees Fahrenheit), while that of the coldest month, July, is around 10 degrees Celsius (50 degrees Fahrenheit).

There are no significant rainy or dry seasons, and the daily weather is variable. Winter rains are most frequent but autumn rains are heaviest, the average rainfall being about 890 millimetres (35 inches). In the region of Punta del Este, violent rainstorms and thunderstorms occur, when the *pamperos* (cool winds from the southern Argentine *pampas*) move north and meet warm tropical air.

The Youngest Country

The discovery of the River Plate estuary and the land of Uruguay is generally attributed to Juan Diaz de Solis, an explorer working for the Spanish crown in 1516. Following the discovery of the Americas by Columbus in 1492, several expeditions had been sent to the New World. They had two objectives. One was to colonize and settle in the New World lands, rich in silver and precious metals; the other was to continue to search for a route through to the Spice Islands and the Indies of the Pacific Ocean.

It was while searching for this route that de Solis entered the River Plate, believing that he might find a way through to the ocean in the west. He never succeeded. He and half a dozen men left his ship to explore the territory that is today Uruguay. And they were ambushed, killed and (according to some accounts) eaten by the native Charrua Indians.

De Solis certainly led the first Spanish expedition into the River Plate. He named it Rio Santa Maria but, after his death, it was called the Rio de Solis. It is possible, however, that he was not the discoverer of the river. It may be that the first ships to enter the estuary were from an earlier expedition, in 1501.

The Charrua Indians are probably unfairly described as cannibals. They were primitive hunters and, to a lesser extent, fishermen. They are known to be related to the tribes of Patagonia in southern Argentina. They were described as being very tall, with broad copper-coloured faces, straight coarse hair and a sad, resigned expression. Writing of Indians seen in 1531, one contemporary chronicler observed that: "their canoes were...beautifully worked...with very long paddles decorated by crests and tassels of feathers on the handles." Like most Indians of the southern plains, the Charrua were fierce and formidable warriors. They would make surprise attacks on their enemies, shouting warlike cries. After the battle, they would collect the skulls of their victims, from which they made ceremonial drinking-cups.

Exploration of the Rio de Solis continued, particularly when it became evident that it provided a route to the silver-rich countries of Peru and Bolivia. Another explorer, the navigator Cabot, was the first to bring pieces of silver down the river. From that time, the Rio de Solis became known as the Rio de la Plata—"the Silver River"—and hence (in English) the River Plate. With the increasing use of the waterway, settlement began along its shores. The town of Asuncion, now the capital of Paraguay, was founded upriver on the west bank. And, in 1545, the first small herd of European cattle to enter the River Plate

Sebastian Cabot, the first man to bring pieces of silver down the Rio de Solis. This led to the river being re-named the Rio de la Plata (Silver River)—hence its English name of the River Plate

region was driven from the coast all the way to Asuncion. It was not until the early years of the seventeenth century that Hernando Arias, the Governor of the River Plate region, shipped one hundred cattle and one hundred horses across the River Uruguay to the "east bank", where they were left to run wild and breed.

A few years later the first missionaries arrived in the "east bank"—Franciscans in the north, Jesuits in the south. They managed to pacify some of the Charrua Indians who, until then, had resisted all attempts of colonization. Following the herds and the missionaries, came nomadic *gauchos* (cowboys) from the west bank of the river, to hunt and kill the cattle for their hides. They, in turn, were followed by merchants from Buenos Aires, now the capital of Argentina, but then only a small military outpost. From these beginnings, grew the large *estancias* (ranches) for which Uruguay has become famous.

The Spaniards had established themselves on the east bank of the river with considerable interests in the region when, in 1680, a Portuguese expedition arrived. The Portuguese built a settlement on the north shore, at Colonia del Sacramento, on the opposite side of the river to Buenos Aires. The Spaniards were forced to take action. They could not allow the Portuguese to interfere with the prosperous trade in hides and in the contraband traffic of the River Plate. And so began almost 150 years of conflict between the Spanish and Portuguese colonists,

A modern view of the River Plate at Colonia del Sacramento, where the Portuguese established a settlement in 1680

over a territory inhabited mainly by growing numbers of cattle.

During the eighteenth century, more and more *criollo* cattlemen moved from the "west bank" to the "east bank" of the River Uruguay. (The name *criollo* is given to people born in South America who are of mixed Spanish and Indian descent.) In 1726, the Spaniards built a fortress on the spot where the town of Montevideo later developed. They were always aware of the Portuguese to the north, who were trying to push their frontier southwards to the banks of the River Plate. Towards the end of the century, the Spaniards' position was seriously threatened. Because Spain was occupied in Europe with a war against England, it became more difficult to exert authority over distant colonies. At the same time, the English fleet had established control of the seas and could, with relative ease, disrupt communications between Spain and South America.

In 1806, the British attempted to overthrow the Spaniards in South America by capturing Buenos Aires. They were almost successful, but, at the last minute, the *criollo* population rejected the authority of the British as being little different to that of Spain. They had no wish to replace one colonial power with another. The British retreated to Montevideo which, after a bloody battle leaving many dead, they occupied for seven months. The local people had already had some experience of the British, when some years earlier the passengers of two ships found themselves stranded in Montevideo. The women convicts from one ship and the missionaries from the other were a strange

General Auchmuty, under whose command the British occupied Montevideo for seven months in 1806

but curiously successful mix, and many decided to remain in the "east bank". To add to their number, many entrepreneurs had set sail from Britain on hearing of the attempt to take Buenos Aires. They too now came to Montevideo, ready to sell the goods they had brought from English factories.

Under the gentle but firm authority of the British General Auchmuty, captors and captives got on well together. Trade goods were actively exchanged; so too were new ideas and philosophies. A weekly newspaper was printed in English and Spanish, and word spread of Bonaparte's victories in Spain. The talk was of democracy and independence. The British occupation came to an end when more supplies and troops arrived for a second, although disastrous, attempt on Buenos

Aires. Defeated, the troops were forced to make a shamefaced departure for home. Many, however, chose to disobey their military orders and remained in the "east bank" for the rest of their lives.

The course was now firmly set for a move towards independence. When the Spanish Viceroy of Buenos Aires was deposed in 1810, it became only a matter of time before the "east bank" would be free. All over South America, countries were breaking away from the authority of Spain. But it took the future country of Uruguay longer than expected, because of its strategic situation between the two great powers of Brazil and Argentina. Uruguay's fight for independence was complicated by the attempts of both Spanish Argentina and Portuguese Brazil to annexe the territory for themselves. At different times, the "east bank" would find itself backed by either of these great countries, against the other, while at other times the people also fought between themselves. Montevideo became a centre of anarchy and strife.

One man arose above the confusion and was responsible, more than any other, for the successful emergence of the independent Republic of Uruguay. He was Jose Gervasio Artigas, himself a skilled horseman, whose army comprised ill-equipped *gauchos,* Indians from the former Jesuit missions, bandits, cut-throats and some loyal townsmen. Artigas was determined not to submit to either of his powerful neighbours. Equally, he recognized that he could not go into battle against both at the same time.

A statue of Jose Gervasio Artigas, in Montevideo. He was the most influential figure in the emergence of the independent Republic of Uruguay

His answer was to lead a mass exodus of people from the "east bank", across the River Uruguay, into exile on the west-bank territory of Argentina. For two months, an incongruous crocodile of ox-carts, pack-mules, cattle, horses, men, women and children trekked across the plains and hills, in the heat and dust of summer. No less than 16,000 people followed Artigas. From their retreat on the other side of the river, they began a campaign of harrassment, guerrilla tactics and terrorism against the armies in the "east bank". They had few weapons. Some of the lucky ones carried muskets and swords, but the majority had simply knives, or *boleadores*—weapons used by *gauchos* for catching animals.

In 1813, Artigas's army left its exile to help in the siege of Montevideo. The Spaniards were thrown out but quarrels ensued between the people of the "east bank" and the *criollos* from Buenos Aires who had helped them in the siege. Artigas was the country's undisputed leader, but he wanted no part in the squabbles. Once again, he led his army upcountry. He denounced the Buenos Aires government and it declared him a traitor.

His fame had now spread far and wide. His following came from a region far greater than the land of modern Uruguay. Several provinces in Argentina gave him their allegiance. And this was part of his great dream. He envisaged not just independence for the "east bank" but a federation of the

A statue of Juan Antonio Lavelleja, another important figure in the struggle for "east bank" independence

provinces of the River Plate, with himself as the "Protector of Free Peoples".

But it was not to be. The Spaniards having been defeated, it was now the turn of the Portuguese Brazilians to invade the war-torn territory. And, at his back, the Buenos Aires government were trying to regain from Artigas the provinces it had lost to him. The odds were overwhelming. Artigas was forced to retreat beyond the River Uruguay and into Paraguay where he lived in exile for thirty years, until he died in 1850.

Whilst the Portuguese occupied the "east bank" for the next five years, the fight for freedom inspired by Artigas was taken up by exiles in Argentina who plotted and waited. Their moment eventually came in 1825. Just thirty-three men—the famous "Immortal Thirty-Three", led by Juan Antonio Lavalleja, crossed the River Uruguay and entered the "east bank", where their countrymen were waiting for them. Together, and with the backing of the Argentine government, they headed for Montevideo. The Portuguese in Brazil reacted immediately and sent a fleet to blockade the River Plate. And the two great countries found themselves at war with each other.

This was a situation which the British government feared, because it would disrupt trade in the region. Pressure was brought to bear on the two sides by the British Foreign Office, and they were persuaded to recognize Uruguay as an independent nation. In 1828, the new nation of the Republica Oriental del Uruguay was created—the youngest Spanish-speaking state in the South American continent.

A Welfare State

From the time of independence until 1903, when Jose Batlle y Ordonez became President, Uruguay experienced twenty-five changes of government. Of these, only three were able to complete their term without apparent opposition or interruption. Ten survived one or more revolutions, nine were ousted from power, two Presidents were assassinated and one was seriously injured. It was amazing that, at the end of all this chaos and violence, the country could be transformed into a peaceful and progressive state, under the wise leadership of Batlle y Ordonez. That the Republic of Uruguay would become South America's first "welfare state"—a model of order and democracy—was, to say the least, remarkable.

The first two decades were dominated by the rivalry between two leading generals—Rivera and Oribe—who earlier had fought together for independence. These men challenged each other for the highest office in the country. They took their rivalry to the battlefield and it is reported that General Oribe rode a

A political banner for the Blancos. The people of Uruguay have been divided into Blancos (Whites) and Colorados (Reds) ever since the troubled early years of Uruguayan independence

white horse, and his lancers carried white pennons on their spearheads. For this reason, they were called the Blancos (Whites). The followers of Rivera, who rode a bay horse, had red pennons. So they were called the Colorados (Reds). From that time, the people of Uruguay have been divided into Whites and Reds (Blancos and Colorados).

At first, this division had no political significance; but, in time, the Whites became the country party, the Reds the town party. The Whites were the Church party; the Reds were anticlerical.

Argentina mostly gave support to the Whites; Brazil to the Reds. Other foreign powers, including France and England, were drawn into the struggle. Antagonism between these groups led to civil war from 1839 to 1851, during which time Montevideo was under siege for nine years. Even then, the fighting did not stop. In 1865, Uruguay was committed, alongside Brazil and Argentina, in a war against Paraguay. By the 1870s, the military had stepped in and while they governed the country it enjoyed a degree of peace and stability. Even so, as late as 1880, on resigning the presidency, Colonel Latorre is quoted as saying that the Uruguayans were ungovernable.

The strife, wars and chaos delayed any attempts to develop the country. At the time of independence, Uruguay had scarcely 74,000 inhabitants: its main economic resources—livestock and land—belonged to a few families who had acquired vast estates in the countryside during the colonial period. Even so, the herds of cattle had been greatly reduced during the years of warfare.

But Montevideo, which in the 1820s was said to be a "sad and half-abandoned town......with ruined ramparts, broken-up streets, dirty and decayed habitations", soon came back to life. This was largely due to its position as a trading-post on the River Plate, which had attracted a large number of Europeans to live there. The population in 1843 was said to be 15,000 Europeans and 11,000 Uruguayans. Local shipping was controlled by Italians. Retail trades (textiles, leather, furnishing, dressmaking and hairdressing) were in the hands of the French, Lebanese, Jewish and Armenian people. The

The port of Montevideo in 1850. By the mid-nineteenth century, Montevideo was a thriving commercial centre

skilled labourers were people who had come from many parts of Europe. The import and export firms and warehouses were chiefly British.

The interior of the country, however, was almost totally neglected. Only a small amount of land was under cultivation and the ranch-owners did little to improve their estates. Some immigrants chose to grow crops and vegetables near to Montevideo, but the native Uruguayans disliked this kind of farming. They preferred the pastoral life. Pedigree sheep were imported from England from about the middle of the nineteenth century, and good quality wool became an important item in the economy. But it was many years before landowners or speculators felt sufficiently confident to invest in the country.

As the threat of revolution and instability ebbed, so development was begun, albeit slowly. There were no roads outside the towns and no bridges. Rivers had to be crossed on horseback. So railways, when they were built, were most effective and welcome. They were constructed largely with British capital, and they began to open up the country. Although, in his later years, Garibaldi had written that he feared the day when "steam and iron will come to increase the riches of the Uruguayan soil", he need not have worried. The railways were an essential element in the development of the interior of the republic. By 1910, the total length of railways in operation was, relative to the size of the Republic, greater than in any other country in South America. There was now a direct

An early steam locomotive, still running today. In the late nineteenth century the railways did much to end Uruguay's isolation

connection from Montevideo to most of the ports on the River Uruguay.

In line with other South American countries, Uruguay looked to foreign capital and investment to help with development. European and American companies soon made their presence felt. The earliest electric-light plant was installed in Montevideo in 1886; it was the first to be set up in South America. Montevideans revelled in the novelty of the street lighting that was introduced soon afterwards; and even private houses were wired. The telephone was first tried in Montevideo in 1878. By the 1890s, Montevideo had more telephones per head than any other city in South America.

One foreign company made history in the meat business. In 1863, a German named G.C. Giebert started producing meat-extract in Uruguay, based on the process invented fifteen years earlier by Baron Justus von Liebig. Conditions were good and the business flourished. By 1864, he had made his first exports. In 1865, he built the world's first meat-extract factory at the small port of Fray Bentos on the River Uruguay. In the following year, the Liebig's Extract of Meat Company was formed in London. From the start it was a profitable business. Production of the meat-extract complemented the traditional jerked beef. This was beef which was salted and dried—the only known way of preserving meat until refrigeration was introduced on land and sea.

In the last quarter of the nineteenth century, as a result of immigration from the Mediterranean countries, the population more than doubled, rising from 450,000 people to about one million in 1900. The newcomers brought with them books and fashionable ideas from Europe which were to change Uruguay.

At the time in Uruguay, there were no laws to protect workers, and very few people received any form of schooling. The first major reform to be introduced, which met with opposition from the conservative authorities and the Church, was free education for all. The man responsible for carrying through the legislation was Jose Pedro Varela, who is now considered a national hero. His achievements were made possible by the unlikely support of the military dictator of the time, Colonel Latorre.

Another reformer, who chose to spread the word through his own newspaper, was (President) Jose Batlle y Ordonez. Born in 1856, he was thirty years old when he founded *El Dia,* a newspaper that it still widely-read today. At the turn of the century, the running of the country was again disrupted by strife and assassination. Just one year after becoming President, in 1903, Batlle y Ordonez was faced by a Blanco revolt which lasted for eight months. He defeated his opponents, and his victory was very significant for the future of the country. It was followed by a reorganization of political parties, and a long period of international peace and orderly government for Uruguay.

Jose Batlle y Ordonez was twice elected President of Uruguay, from 1903 to 1907 and from 1911 to 1915. He refused to disregard the constitution and succeed himself. He spent the interim four years (between his two terms of office) in Europe, acquainting himself with different methods of government and social reform. When he became President for the second time, he introduced reforms that made Uruguay the most advanced welfare state in South America. Batlle y Ordonez was a thoughtful, energetic man, and few doubted his sincerity.

Many of the reforms he began were written into the "workingman's charter" of the 1950s. This allowed for a working week of forty-eight hours, a compulsory rest-day after five days work, a minimum wage, a free medical service, old-age pensions, compensation for discharged workers, and unemployment pay. He also introduced legislation to protect illegitimate children, to abolish capital punishment and to make bull-fighting illegal. He believed that the State should own the country's major industries, and so he nationalized the telephone and electricity services, as well as the railways.

He reduced the power of the Catholic Church, separating its functions from those of the State. As a result, schools were not required to give religious instruction, people did not have to get married in church, and divorce was made legal.

Batlle y Ordonez was the right man in the right place at the right time. It is doubtful that any other man could have taken Uruguay so successfully out of the nineteenth century and into the twentieth. He did have his critics and his enemies, particularly among the conservatives and the wealthy who were affected by his policies. But the strength of his character, message and memory lies in his continued influence throughout the twentieth century, long after his death.

Government House in Montevideo

There was, however, one reform in which he was not so successful: he sought to abolish the office of president and replace it with government by committee. The proposal was not popular among the opposition; consequently, in his own lifetime, he had to accept a compromise of joint government by the President and a National Council of Administration.

Since his death, the government of Uruguay has alternated between the two, depending on the President and party in power, and the constitution has been changed several times. The argument has become one of the dominant issues in Uruguayan political life, and an important contributory factor in the economic and social unrest that has faced the country in recent years.

The constitution of 1967 laid down the principal features of government and these did not change until 1973 when the armed forces seized power and closed Congress. It confirmed the right of every person, male or female, of eighteen years or over to vote. It also stated that there would be a General Assembly comprising a Chamber of Representatives and a Senate. The Chamber of Representatives would have ninety-nine members elected from all nineteen departments in the country, the minimum age of deputies being twenty-five. The Senate would have thirty-one members, each elected for four years, who must be at least thirty years of age. The General Assembly would elect the five members of the Supreme Court of Justice, which was responsible for the entire judicial system.

The City that is a Nation

Nowhere in the world does a city dominate a nation's life, as does Montevideo in Uruguay. Commercially, industrially, politically and culturally, it is the centre of the country. Montevideo is on the northern shore of the River Plate, 120 kilometres (75 miles) upstream from the Atlantic Ocean. It covers an area of 400 square kilometres (150 square miles). And almost half the country's population of 2.95 million live in the city. The number is increasing rapidly as people come from the rural areas to settle in the city, where they hope to find work.

In the twentieth century Montevideo has developed rapidly, largely due to the government's action to improve and enlarge the port facilities in 1901. Before that time, ships had to discharge their cargo in the harbour onto lighters. Once the port was modernized, however, large ocean-going vessels could dock for loading and unloading. Today, the port of Montevideo handles the vast bulk of Uruguay's foreign trade: almost ninety per cent of all imports and exports pass through it.

A meat-processing factory in Montevideo. Most of Uruguay's modern industries are located in the capital

Most of the country's modern industries are in the city. There are wool-processing and meat-packing plants, textile and leather factories, and businesses producing wines and dairy products. ANCAP (Administracion Nacional de Combustibles, Alcohol y Portland) oil refineries, cement-works, railway workshops and the electric-power system are all concentrated in the city.

Montevideo is also the seat of government, as well as the only city in which higher education is available, at the University of the Republic (Universidad de La Republica), founded in 1849.

The country's transport network radiates from Montevideo, with over 3,200 kilometres (2,000 miles) of railway competing with 12,900 kilometres (8,000 miles) of road. As Uruguay is a small, compact territory with no difficult terrain, it has been relatively easy to connect Montevideo with the rural areas. But, whereas the streets of the city are filled with vehicles of every kind, outside the city, heading north, the roads are empty. It is possible to drive for hours without seeing any other vehicle.

The city is served by the main international airport, Carrasco, from which regular services of the state airline, PLUNA, connect Montevideo with other cities of South America, and with Europe. There is also a hydrofoil service across the River Plate to Buenos Aires, in Argentina.

Montevideo was founded in 1726 by Bruno Mauricio de Zabala, a governor of Buenos Aires. It was part of the Spanish campaign to fight off the Portuguese, who were advancing from Brazil. The "Cerro" (hill) which stands behind the city had been known to sailors many years earlier as a landmark where they would find the beautiful natural harbour, a haven from their long journeys across the oceans. It is claimed that the city owes its name to one of the crew on Magellan's expedition in the early sixteenth century who, on seeing a form of land on a distant horizon, shouted *"Monte vide eu!"*—"I see a hill!" The Cerro, 118 metres (about 400 feet) high, has on its summit an old fort which is now a military museum. On top of the fort is the oldest lighthouse in the country (dating from 1804). It is still a welcome sight to merchant ships, tankers and vessels returning from Antarctica.

During its early years, Montevideo was mostly a Spanish garrison town, occupying a riverside headland where today narrow streets and one-story houses represent Montevideo's colonial heritage. Although the original fortifications have been destroyed, and few of the buildings were built earlier than the late eighteenth or early nineteenth century, this part of the city still retains a colonial atmosphere. Known as the Old City, this is the financial and business heart of Uruguay where the stock exchange, the Bank of the Republic, the rambling Customs House and all the head offices of banks, shipping firms, and import and export houses are to be found. Here, too, is the Plaza Constitucion—the oldest square in the city—with the cathedral (1790-1804) on one side, and the town hall (1804-1810) on the other.

Part of the Old City of Montevideo, which still retains much of its colonial heritage

The statue of Jose Gervasio Artigas in the centre of Montevideo's main square, the Plaza Independencia

In the late 1800s and early 1900s, when many immigrants were arriving from Europe to settle in the city, they influenced styles of building with a more ornate form of architecture which became the fashion in the newer commercial and residential districts that developed on the border of the old quarter. Calle Sarandi, a narrow shopping street, connects the old Plaza Constitucion with the newer Plaza Independencia, Montevideo's main square. In the centre of Plaza Independencia is a statue of the national hero Jose Gervasio Artigas, above an underground mausoleum. The square is surrounded by colonnaded buildings with Government House on the southern side. And, facing Artigas, is the Palacio Salvo—the city's first skyscraper.

As there was no lack of space surrounding the city, beautiful parks have been created, and many avenues are wide and lined with trees. Leading off the Plaza Independencia is the busy Avenida 18 de julio, with its shops, street-traders, theatres, cafés and offices. As the climate in Montevideo is temperate, with only a moderate rainfall, outdoor cafés are part of the way of life and the pavements of the Avenida 18 de julio are always thronged. Europeans slip into life in Montevideo with ease, as the European heritage comes through clearly in Uruguayan life. One custom, among the wealthier people of Montevideo, is meeting for afternoon tea in a *confiteria* (tea-shop) where the windows are filled with elaborate cream cakes, reminiscent of Austria and Germany.

Visitors to the city should, though, temporarily leave this

One of the many small tree-lined squares which help to make Montevideo such an attractive city

bustling atmosphere, to walk from the Avenida 18 de julio, along Avenida del Libertador Brig. Gen. Juan Lavalleja (also known as Avenida Agraciada)—which is the city's most modern showplace—to the marble Legislative Palace. This is the most lavish public building in Uruguay. Its ornate columned facade is one of the grandest in all South America.

A large proportion of the area of Montevideo has been devoted to parks. They are an impressive feature of the city. The design of many of them was influenced by French landscape-gardeners of the late eighteenth and early nineteenth centuries. The Prado is the oldest. Amongst its rolling lawns, trees, lakes and grottoes, which are a delight to wander through, is a magnificent rose garden planted with 850 varieties. The largest and most popular

Montevideo's Legislative Palace. Built of marble, this is one of the grandest buildings in all South America

Belloni's statue *La Carreta*, which shows a traditional peasant waggon drawn by three yoke of oxen

park is the Rodo, which has a boating lake and a children's playground. No visitor can fail to be impressed by the immense sculptures and statues which adorn most of Montevideo's parks.

One of the most remarkable statues is *La Carreta* by Belloni in the Batlle y Ordonez Park. It shows, life-size in bronze, three yoke of oxen drawing a waggon, depicting the type of transport used by Uruguayan peasants before the age of the railway and of motor traffic. It is a favourite with visitors, watched by a sharp-eyed guard, always ready to chase young enthusiasts bent on riding the waggon. In another park is Belloni's *La Diligence,* a full-size stage-coach and horses. Another striking sculpture

***The Gaucho,* a bronze sculpture by Jose Luis Zorilla**

is Prati's *The Last of the Charruas,* in memory of the now-extinct native Indian people, wiped out when colonists and settlers took over their lands.

Among other monuments, Montevideo is the proud possessor of one of the two bronze versions of Michelangelo's *David,* which can be seen outside the municipal building, as well as the bronze cast sculpture by Jose Luis Zorilla—*The Gaucho*—which commemorates all the *gauchos* who lived and died for their country.

Montevideo is one of the cultural centres of South America. It has been called "the Athens of La Plata". The city's first theatre was the Casa de Comedias opened in 1795, while the Solis Theatre, inaugurated in 1856, is still in use today. Drama and literature have always tended to the romantic in Uruguay, with the *gaucho* as the central figure of much nostalgia and poetry. Juan Zorilla de San Martin, father of the sculptor of *The Gaucho,* was Uruguay's first notable writer. He was known as "the poet of the fatherland". He concentrated on the legends, history and heroes of his homeland; his masterpiece, *Tabare,* is an epic poem about the South American Indians.

Montevideo has two symphony orchestras and several chamber music orchestras, as well as a variety of museums and libraries, and art galleries exhibiting the work of native and

The Solis Theatre, which has been in continuous use for well over one hundred years. It was inaugurated in 1856

foreign artists. The Uruguayan Pedro Figari (1861-1938) is one of the greatest South American artists.

The people of Montevideo also like to go to the cinema. Many international films are shown, and both cinema and theatre are widely discussed in the press. Montevideo has four television channels and twenty-five radio stations.

The first printing press appeared in Montevideo with the British invaders in 1807. The first newspaper, *The Southern Star,* was printed on it. There are now five Montevideo newspapers and most have an allegiance to one of the political parties. They include *El Dia,* the Batlle y Ordonez newspaper. Because transport to the rest of the country is relatively easy, papers printed in the city can be distributed in all except the remotest regions on the day of publication. As a result, there are no important provincial newspapers. This is yet another way in which the capital dominates the rest of the country.

Like all South Americans, Uruguayans love football. Their main stadium, the Centenario, was constructed in Montevideo in 1930 for the first Football World Cup. The hosts emerged on that occasion as victors and World Champions, a feat which Uruguay has achieved three times since. Montevideo boasts a great variety of sports facilities, including an Olympic swimming pool and a golf-course claimed by some to be the best in America. Horse-racing and show-jumping are also very popular, and the Maronas race-course attracts enormous crowds.

For those Montevideans who prefer less strenuous activities, there are many fine sandy beaches. They extend for fifteen

Pocitos beach, Montevideo

kilometres (ten miles) along the whole of the metropolitan waterfront, joined by a splendid road—the Rambla Naciones Unidas—with sections named in honour of different nations. The beach season is from December to the middle of April, Uruguay's summer, when the locals spend the weekends swimming, sunbathing, yachting and rowing.

Some beaches, like Buceo and Malvin Alto, are surrounded by modern housing estates with complete community facilities, where new suburbs have been developed. One of the main older residential areas is Pocitos. The name, meaning "little holes", is derived from the time when washerwomen used to dig on the bank of the river. The district is well supplied with hotels, restaurants and night-clubs. The streets of Montevideo are tree-lined and attractive. Traffic is never obtrusive, though the Montevideo Shopping Centre—a complex of shops and supermarkets—has in part changed the horizon. Bays, like Carrasco in the east, have lost nothing of their charm, combining parks and forest with long sandy beaches, to retain a quiet, semi-rural atmosphere.

One feature of Montevideo, and also seen throughout the country, are the amazing old cars that line the streets. For vintage car spotters, Uruguay is a paradise. Model T Fords, fifty-year-old Chevrolets and familiar British cars of the nineteen

A 1920s Ford—one of the many vintage cars still in use in Uruguay

fifties are all commonplace. And most have been kept in perfect running order by "cannibalizing" parts from other models, with an abundance of loving care.

The Uruguayan passion for old cars which they call *cachilas,* developed from the economic need forced on people by the high prices of imported new vehicles. But, over the years, owners have come to take a pride in the "veterans". Now, although some may change hands at bargain prices, the *cachilas* are becoming collectors' items. Restrictions on export mean that these historic cars remain a uniquely Uruguayan sight.

The Uruguayans at Work

The people of Uruguay are mostly descended from nineteenth- and twentieth- century immigrants from Spain, Italy and other European countries. A small number of Blacks and *mulattos* (people of mixed Black and Indian blood), perhaps 60,000 altogether, live near the border with Brazil. Some also live in Montevideo. Walking along the streets of the capital, watching people in the shops and in the side-walk cafés the similarity to a European capital is striking.

The original natives, the Charrua Indians, were killed off when first the nomadic *gauchos* and then the Spanish settlers moved in and took over their lands. Some of the British soldiers and sailors who had been involved in fighting before independence also chose to remain in Uruguay. But it was only after 1830 that immigration began on a larger scale. Some 648,000 immigrants entered the country before 1926. Many more might have come had they not been put off by the political factions who were constantly at war. Nevertheless, in the

An old woman (of typically mixed ancestry) with her grandchild

twentieth century, communities have arrived from Central Europe and the Middle East, including Poles, Romanians, Russians, Turks and Lebanese, as well as thousands of Jewish refugees from Germany.

Uruguay has had many advantages to offer the potential immigrant. It is a small country, well supplied with transport facilities in every direction. The land is good; there is hardly an area that is not used for ranching, sheep or agriculture, even in the more remote districts. As a result of the measures of President Batlle y Ordonez in creating the welfare state, workers and their families are well looked after. And the people of

Uruguay are friendly and hospitable. Yet the numbers that have settled are still relatively small, many preferring the bigger, perhaps more sophisticated neighbouring country of Argentina.

A population census was carried out in 1963. It was the first since 1908. From this, with average yearly increases, the present figure of 2.95 million people is deduced. While half the population lives in the city of Montevideo, many thousands more have homes in the nearby department of Canelones. In all, over eighty-one per cent of the population is considered to be urban, living in the towns on the River Plate and along the coast, such as Colonia, San Jose and Maldonado, and in those on the River Uruguay, such as Salto and Paysandu. The remaining nineteen per cent are spread through the rest of the country. The figure for the average density of population is estimated as fourteen per square kilometre (37 per square mile).

The very low annual birth-rate (18.4 per thousand inhabitants) and the very low death-rate (10.6 per thousand), with a life expectancy of sixty-seven years for men and seventy-four years for women, is exceptional among South American countries. So, too, is the age distribution among the population. It is a country where concern for the elderly is an important issue as almost thirteen per cent of the population is over sixty, and twenty-seven per cent is under fifteen, with the remaining sixty per cent between the two. (In Brazil half the population is under twenty-one.)

These statistics may well be accounted for by the Uruguayan attitude to religion. Nominally, the country is Catholic (another legacy of the Spaniards), though there are few religious buildings dating back to the colonial days. With the invasions of the English and then the French, the people of Uruguay were exposed to alternative religious ideas. There was, therefore, not a great deal of opposition when Batlle y Ordonez presided over the separation of the church and state in 1919. Nor was there any objection when religious festivals were changed, and Christmas became "Family Day", with Easter an official seven days' holiday called "Criollo Week", later renamed "Tourist Week". Religion is not taught in the state schools, and there are few churches in the interior of the country. Marriages do not have to take place in church, and a wife can obtain a divorce without having to state her reasons. (Husbands at the moment

The nineteenth-century cathedral of Paysandu. Uruguay is nominally a Roman Catholic country but there is no state religion

do not enjoy the same freedom, although politicians are currently campaigning for it.)

Uruguay is also quite exceptional when compared to other countries in South America in that more than ninety per cent of the population are literate. This is largely due to the work of Varela who, in 1877, introduced free, compulsory primary education for all. Nowadays, secondary education is also compulsory and free, and no fees are payable for university education or for industrial apprenticeship. Over ninety-five per cent of students go to secondary school and almost five per cent attend university. The University of the Republic has schools of humanities, sciences and engineering; and a distinguished school of medicine. The Labour University, made up from a group of technical schools, provides vocational training through industrial and night schools, and for farming occupations through rural schools.

Sadly, in the last twenty-five years, Uruguay's "welfare state" has been badly hit by economic and political problems, and there is a shortage of money, particularly for the Departments of Health and Education. In the past, Uruguayan workers were envied by their South America neighbours for their charter which allowed them free medical treatment, old-age and service pensions, and unemployment pay. But, in practice, the country has been unable to meet its commitments. It is reckoned that there are now, for example, 700,000 pensioners, one to every 1.6 members of the working population. And fifteen per cent of the population are unemployed. Additionally, the

Herding cattle in northern Uruguay. Seventy-five per cent of the land is pasture for herds and flocks

administration of the welfare system has become very cumbersome, with one third of the population employed in government.

While most of the people who have jobs live and work in Montevideo and other towns, the country's main income comes from the countryside, from the cattle and sheep that make up the livestock industry. Such is the value of the meat industry that seventy to seventy-five per cent of the land is pasture for the herds and flocks, with only ten to twelve per cent of the land being used for agriculture. Uruguay relies heavily on these two commodities for its foreign trade. Its success or failure is very dependent on the extent to which other countries can afford to, or need to, buy its goods. Unfortunately for Uruguay, some of the markets it has relied on for many years are no longer there. For example, the E.E.C., once a major meat importer, now exports its own meat. Similarly the U.S.A., once a major woollen goods importer, has cut back the quota it is prepared to take from Uruguay.

Traditionally, Uruguayans have preferred cattle and sheep to agricultural farming, which explains why such a small area of the country is given over to food products, despite the excellent soil. The government is now looking for ways of increasing this production, to make Uruguay grow enough to feed its own people, and perhaps to export as well. The main crops produced are rice, wheat, maize, sugar-beet, sugar-cane, potatoes, sunflower-seeds, sorghum, barley and oats. A visit to one of the markets in Montevideo demonstrates the variety of fruit and

Cultivating sorghum in northern Uruguay. The soil is excellent and efforts are being made to encourage farmers to grow more crops

nuts available: grapes, oranges, lemons, apples, pears, quinces, melons, apricots, figs, chestnuts and almonds. A little further on there are shelves full of locally produced wine, cheese, butter and milk.

Although the country has a superb coastline, and large and rich offshore fishing-grounds, the Uruguayans are not a maritime nation, and the people are not fishermen. Since 1973, an attempt has been made to reverse this situation, and recently small quantities of fish have been exported.

By contrast, Uruguay's seal population has been in demand for over three hundred years, and a sealing industry now operates on the Isla de Lobos, near Punta del Este. It is one of the largest colonies of sea-lions in South America, and the animals are valued for their pelts and oil. Tourists are encouraged to visit the island, as it is one of the few places in the world where the Common Sea-lion *(Otaria bironia* or *jubata)* and the Southern Fur Seal *(Arctocephalus australis)* live side by side.

Tourism is an important part of the Uruguayan economy and a major source of foreign currency. Over one million visitors each year, many from Argentina and Brazil, enjoy the almost perfect climate and the sandy beaches that stretch along the Atlantic coast. Punta del Este, 145 kilometres (about 90 miles) from Montevideo, is the most famous centre. For four months in the summer, the beaches are packed, with sun-shades, bikinis and Coca Cola signs giving the impression of an international resort. Beach bars and a rich scent of grilling meat stamp it as Uruguayan.

Locally-grown fruit on sale in Montevideo

Uruguay has almost no natural raw materials, and the country has no known deposits of coal or petroleum. So industry is dependent on imported raw materials and fuel, especially oil. Recently new hydro-electric plants have been constructed. They now provide over sixty-five per cent of the country's electrical energy needs. Most industries in Uruguay are based on the basic livestock and agricultural economy: meat, textiles and leather. Refrigeration made it possible for Argentina and Uruguay to develop their great modern meat-packing and meat-exporting industries. The plants, or *frigorificos,* prepare canned, frozen and chilled meats, extracts of beef, and many by-products.

Leather is an important product for the manufacture of shoes, gloves, handbags and some clothing. The textile industry was for many years based on wool products. The first mill (La Nacional), established in the 1880s, has now expanded into the production of heavy cotton. Other consumer goods made in Uruguay include tyres, rubber goods and a variety of household appliances.

In the north of the country, some semi-precious stones—agate, amethyst and quartz—are mined. There are also known resources of marble, granite and limestone, the latter being in particular demand for the production of cement. There is also the possibility of natural gas being found, and studies are being

Cans stacked in a meat-processing factory in Montevideo

made to find out whether commercial production of uranium, copper and manganese would be possible.

In these changing times, Uruguay will have to reduce its reliance on imports. Even so, the country is at present also too dependent on world export markets for the sale of its wool and beef. In order to survive, Uruguay may be forced to find ways of creating new industries.

The Gauchos

Of all South American folk heroes, the *gaucho* or cowhand of the southern grasslands of Argentina and Uruguay is the most famous.

In Uruguay today most *gauchos* work in the central and northern regions, where rolling grassland extending from horizon to horizon is broken only by planted groves of eucalyptus trees. The *gaucho* works hard. In summer, the working day begins before dawn and continues until the sun forces a siesta. Then work begins again in the afternoon, until dusk or even later. Round-ups, branding, mending fences, removing parasites from the cattle's skins—all are part of the job. But being a *gaucho* is more than just a job; it is a career, based on a long tradition. Songs, stories and art relate the folklore of the *gaucho* with justifiable pride. These men are held in great respect in Uruguay, but are, in fact, fast disappearing.

In Argentina, *gauchos* first came into being when outlaws, escaping justice in Buenos Aires, fled into the open grasslands.

A *gaucho* forcing a cow into a pen for branding

There, they mixed with the native Indian populations, and learned their skill in capturing and training the wild horses that had escaped from the troops of the Spanish conquistadors in the 1500s. Lawless and nomadic, some *gauchos* moved into Uruguay in the late seventeenth century, following the herds of cattle that had been introduced into the "east bank" in 1603 by Hernando Arias.

Gauchos fought valiantly during the wars of independence. They were brilliant horsemen, at home in the open countryside and able to endure enormous hardship, with little more than a knife or lance for weapons. Charles Darwin, when he met *gauchos* during his visit to Uruguay on the voyage of the *Beagle* in 1832/3, described their ruthlessness.

"With their brightly-coloured garments, great spurs clanking about their heels, and knives stuck as daggers (and often so used) at their waists, they look a very different race of men from what might be expected from their name of *Gauchos,* or simple countrymen. Their politeness is excessive; they never drink their spirits without expecting

***Gauchos* herding cattle into an enclosure**

you to taste it; but whilst making their exceedingly graceful bow, they seem quite as ready, if occasion offered, to cut your throat."

The *gaucho,* as a romantic folk hero, was immortalized some years later in 1872, when Jose Hernandez wrote his epic poem *The Gaucho Martin Fierro.*

"A son am I of the rolling plain
A gaucho born and bred
And this is my pride; to live as free
As the bird that cleaves the sky."

With lines like these, he was recording a fast fading tradition. His words describe the *gaucho* as he will always be remembered, but the reality was different.

Events were occurring in Uruguay and Argentina that would change the *gaucho*'s life for ever. In both countries, much of the vast open grassland was being divided up into *estancias* (ranches) and the *gauchos* no longer wandered "free as the birds". They worked for an *estanciero* (the owner of an *estancia*), in return for food and lodging. The ranches used to be very large, but as the years went by, and land was inherited by different members of a family, they were divided up into smaller and smaller units, so that the *gauchos* now work on small ranches in local areas. The second important event was the arrival of immigrants from Europe. In Argentina particularly, and to a lesser extent in

A *gaucho* vaccinating cattle—another aspect of his varied work

Uruguay, Scots, Irish, English, Italians and Basques became *gauchos!*

In the north and centre of Uruguay, where the tradition is strongest, a *gaucho*'s working dress is a broad-brimmed black hat, long-sleeved cotton shirt, baggy trousers called *bombachas,* and short leather boots. When it is cold he wears a poncho—a square of wool with a slit in the centre to slip his head through. Add an almost obligatory moustache, and the character is complete. There is now a tendency for the younger people to wear jeans and a peaked cap. For special days, however, the

Gauchos* repairing fencing out on the *pampas

gaucho dress is very fine. The *bombachas* are topped with a tight-fitting shirt and hand-embroidered bolero-style jacket, a belt decorated with silver, and a dash of colour from a bright necktie. And the horses have superb hand-tooled leather saddles. To complete his dress, the *gaucho* wears a short knife, sometimes silver-handled, at the belt. It is used for everything—but particularly to cut the barbecued meat which is still the main ingredient of a *gaucho*'s meal.

In his saddlebag, a *gaucho* carries a *mate* (gourd) and silver tube *(bombilla)* with a fine filter at one end from which he drinks. Like most Uruguayans, *gauchos* enjoy the bitter, refreshing (some say stimulating) *yerba* (herb) tea brewed from leaves of a bush related to holly. The leaves are dried and ground to a dust-green powder. When mixed with cold water from a spring, the tea is strongly flavoured. Most people, however, prefer to drink it with hot water.

A hundred years ago, cattle provided *gauchos* with everything they needed. They ate nothing but meat. Milk was very rare—few ranchers thought to use cows for this purpose. And nobody grew vegetables. Leather was extensively used for saddles, clothing, sacks and wineskins. Moistened leather replaced nails, ropes and wire, which were unknown in Uruguay at that time. When Montevideo was founded, the houses, including doors and beds, were constructed of leather.

Also made of leather were the *boleadores* that *gauchos* used for catching animals. *Boleadores* were round stones, wrapped in

A *gaucho* wearing his traditional working clothes

leather and attached to three long rawhide thongs. They were whirled about a *gaucho*'s head and, when thrown, they wrapped around the legs of the pursued animal: a wild horse, or wild cow or perhaps the ostrich-like rhea which is now protected by conservation laws. The place of the *boleadores* has now been taken by the lasso. The *gaucho* uses his rawhide lasso by tying one end to an iron ring behind his saddle, while he holds several coils, which he throws. In this way, the lasso can be aimed as much as ten metres (about 35 feet) away with great accuracy.

A typical ranch is set within a grove of high trees, usually eucalyptus. At or near the gate is a small house, brick or adobe, often with a thatched roof. This is the home of one of the *puesteros,* (pasture-tenders), whose duty it is to look after one of the large pastures and to keep the gate. The white-washed ranch buildings stand out between the trees. There are the barns for shearing and possibly storing the wool, stables for horses, and sheds for cattle; small houses for the labourers, and lastly the house of the ranch-owner himself. This may be large but, if old, it is usually a rambling, roomy, one-storey brick building, plastered on the outside and roofed with tiles.

A modern *estancia* house may be two-storey with broad balconies to give shade. Whatever the style, the house will be surrounded by trees—oranges, peaches, apricots, and other fruit—with a garden of flowers and vegetables. If the ranch is large, there may also be a schoolroom for the children. They dress in smart white overalls, a uniform worn by schoolchildren throughout South America.

A typical white-washed *estancia* (ranch) surrounded by trees

In north and central Uruguay, an average *estancia* is between 1,000 and 2,000 hectares (2,500 and 5,000 acres), and may manage four or five hundred cows and up to six hundred sheep. The fields are divided by wire fences or low banks of trees, with shrubs forming crude hedges. Gates are often simply constructed of wire and poles—much like a section of fence that can be drawn taut across an opening, using a pole for leverage. Much of the success of an *estancia* depends on the *gauchos*.

From time to time, when a herd is moved long distances to market or to the slaughterhouse, the *gauchos* drive the cattle long

***Gauchos* driving a herd of cattle across the grasslands**

distances across the gently rolling countryside. Auctions and sales of sheep and cattle take place on *estancias* and in towns. They provide an occasion for all the farmers in the neighbourhood to get together. Usually, these events are the occasion for an *asado,* or massive barbecue, for which the cattlemen are famous.

Similarly, a common weekend sight at the roadsides, are simple metal barbecue grills, fed with charcoal, on which meat of all types is cooked. The meat is often basted with a mixture of olive oil, delicate herbs and salt to give a mild aromatic flavour. While meat and meat products are almost the universal food, so too is the accompanying salad of fine tomatoes, lettuce or onions.

Gaucho country is notable for its wildlife. Many of the landowners have become strict conservationists, particularly as most surviving wildlife species do not affect the cattle. These endless pastures are home to the rhea, a South American ostrich-like bird. Groups of flightless rhea live in the cattle pastures and wander unmolested by the activity around them. They form a nest on the open ground, several females laying eggs which are guarded and incubated by a single male.

Rheas—these flightless, ostrich-like birds are a common sight on Uruguay's grasslands

A burrowing owl, perched on a fence-post

Far smaller, yet just as conspicuous, are tiny burrowing owls that are about in the daytime. They have a quick flight and move in pairs from post to post along the fences as the cattle are herded by, though they seem unconcerned by the shouting and goading of the *gauchos*.

For the daytime traveller, there are many species of birds to watch: lapwings, red crowned cardinals, vultures, flycatchers and the ubiquitous ovenbird (so-called because of its bulky, rock-hard nest resembling a clay oven). At night, the mammals, like the armadillos and foxes, venture out. While most of the mammals are small, an antlered pampas deer has survived in some places, particularly in the centre of the country where herds are protected by thoughtful ranch-owners.

Gone are the days when *gauchos* had to live off the land, when leather from the rhea made fine shoes, or its plumes were turned into feather-dusters. The romance of bygone times lingers but, for the most part, it is the *gaucho*'s skill with animals that remains unchallenged in a country whose economic mainstay is meat.

Along the River Uruguay

Two small banks (Martin Garcia and Timoteo Dominguez) in the mouth of the River Uruguay were for many years a point of argument between tiny Uruguay and her powerful neighbour Argentina. In every other way, the River Uruguay creates a perfect natural frontier. It has seen few disputes over the years, and has provided a fine waterway for shipping. Now, through hydro-electricity, the river is also providing energy for both countries.

At its mouth, the Uruguay is over 19.3 kilometres (12 miles) wide. It empties alongside the River Parana into the large estuary of the River Plate. Colonia del Sacramento, Uruguay's oldest town which was founded in 1680 by the Portuguese who came from Brazil, is on the River Plate and it makes a convenient starting-point for a journey. Early settlers recognized the strategic position of the headland, now marked by a lighthouse, where the Uruguayan bank turns sharply north-west. Over the years, the Uruguayans have preserved and restored

A view of the River Uruguay, which forms a natural boundary between Uruguay and her more powerful neighbour Argentina

much of what they call the historic quarter of the town. Quiet tree-lined squares are bounded by fine houses.

Visitors from all over Uruguay and from Argentina visit Colonia, as it is the crossing-point of a ferry to Buenos Aires. Small restaurants, craft shops and local artists have a high season in the summer when tourists head for Uruguayan beaches. Otherwise, Colonia offers year-round relaxation. Anglers fish from the jetty and between casts, sip *yerba mate* tea through their silver *bombillas* (straws).

Carmelo, a small town a short distance to the north, is even quieter than Colonia, seeming to come alive only in the summer when it becomes a yachting haven. But Carmelo can be said to be at the mouth of the river; and upstream, as the banks come

Part of the old fortifications and the lighthouse at Colonia on the River Plate

closer, the River Uruguay serves as a highway offering a waterway as far as Paysandu, over 200 kilometres (124.3 miles) further on. On the way, the country on each side is low. Pampas grass fills banks and level places alike with its large white heads and, in summer, myriads of insects gather at darkness around any light.

Above Carmelo, the river is tied to Uruguayan history in two places. Some 20 kilometres (12.4 miles) away is the historic beach of La Agraciada where a statue of General Lavalleja commemorates the famous landing on April 19, 1825 of the thirty-three patriots who went on to secure independence for Uruguay. Beyond Paysandu, the next major town, the river on the Uruguayan side has cut a steep bank beneath a rocky tableland, which bears the name of Artigas because General Artigas once lived at this spot. It is now surmounted by a tall column bearing a bust of the general. The river narrows at this point and forms whirlpools at the rapids of El Hervidero. The historic site is now in the care of the Department of Parks and Countryside.

Along this stretch of the river, there are increasing signs of the meat, leather and sugar industries. One port, Fray Bentos, 402 kilometres (250 miles) from Montevideo, has a name which many Britons still associate with a famous brand of corned beef. Hundreds of thousands of tonnes of processed meat in cans have been exported from this town, and canning remains its principal industry, with exports now to other countries.

Fishing from the jetty at Colonia

Inland, roads run parallel to the river on both sides with few interruptions. As if to give variety or express their wishful thinking, the Uruguayans add STEEP HILL signs to what most Europeans see as gentle slopes. But signs are appreciated, especially those for bends which appear unexpectedly; or for unguarded railway crossings, as the track crosses from field to field. Just occasionally, some vintage steam locomotive will rumble across the way, pulling a train of farm waggons—the major *estancias* have individual "halts" and sidings.

One should never be surprised in South America to hear an unusual language or accent. The space and opportunity offered by the sub-continent have always attracted immigrants, and the land around Paysandu is no exception. At San Javier, a small village beside the river, the population comprises mainly families with Russian names. The people left their homeland many years ago though even now, several generations later, their life follows the agricultural pattern of Europe. Long, four-wheeled carts are drawn by pairs of horses, and raise dust as they clatter through a village street. This could be a scene from somewhere bordering the Danube. Even the fishermen on the river use rowing-boats that could be straight from the Danube Delta. These people work the fields and build houses with a spirit of family enterprise that has given them hope in a new land.

From Paysandu a bridge gives the first road link with Argentina. During the summer and at holiday weekends, many Argentinians visit the springs of Guaviyu where water pours

A descendant of Russian immigrants in the village of San Javier

from the ground at 39 degrees Celsius. Like most hot springs, the waters are believed to possess curative properties. Young and old alike spend hours in specially built pools or beneath fast-flowing showers. As camping is a major national pastime of Uruguayans and Argentinians, entire families set their tents by the river. People fish, cook enormous open-air barbecues and simply laze in the sun. Guaviyu appears suddenly as an incongruous interruption to what is otherwise gently rolling land dotted with eucalyptus groves and scattered palms.

Paysandu marks a distinct narrowing of the river, while inland the gently rolling countryside hardly changes, except that the

The thermal springs at Guaviyu—the baths are popular with both Uruguayans and visitors from neighbouring Argentina

climate hints at the tropics, and the grasslands are broken by palm savannahs or extensive stands of tall palms. Parrots and parakeets in noisy flocks wing their way from tree to tree. Large, colourful butterflies visit an abundance of flowers and it is not surprising to find long rows of citrus trees spreading across the countryside. Salto, the next large town, is the centre for the production of oranges, and the fruit is transported from there across Uruguay by truck.

By Salto, literally meaning "jump" or "leap", the River Uruguay too, changes. Here the current is quicker and the river crashes over a series of rocky shelves. People fish, standing precariously among the rapids or working small boats upstream in the fast water. They are usually hoping for a dorado, one of the best game fish, which average seven kilograms (over fifteen pounds) in weight and are excellent eating.

For the people of Salto, rowing is a favourite pastime. The sport is not just a passing craze. The dining room of the Rowers Club has shelves lined with silver cups, reminders of challenges with other clubs along the river.

At one time larger rapids blocked the River Uruguay, upstream from Salto. But since its completion in 1981, the new Salto Grande Dam has spanned the river, eliminating the rapids and forming a lake stretching over 150 kilometres (93.2 miles) upstream. This courageous project was undertaken jointly by Uruguay and Argentina. The two countries began in the 1940s with an agreement and formation of a special commission. The

Palm savannah bordering on the River Uruguay

The hydro-electric dam near Salto. This provides a road and rail bridge between Uruguay and Argentina and is also a useful source of power for the two countries

dam provides a road and rail bridge across the river, and power for both countries. For the foreseeable future, Uruguay will not need all its share of the power and so is "selling" the energy to its neighbour. Huge pylons support long cables spanning the river from country to country.

This new lake is destined to be a fisherman's paradise. Special channels have been built into the dam to allow migrating fish to move up and down river. The fish are counted automatically as they pass through the dam, and a computer analyzes the number of each individual species. Eventually, the research will help determine productive methods of "fish-farming" for the lake and, later, commercial exploitation. The lake itself has risen to the edge of the eucalyptus groves and has become an attraction for boating and rowing enthusiasts.

Once mature, the Salto Grande Lake will become the centrepiece in the nearest Uruguay can get to a tropical zone. Being influenced by the climate of the interior, the gently rolling hills and rich grassland are home to snakes and huge lizards.

Close to the frontier with Brazil, the River Uruguay becomes narrower and its banks higher, as it issues from the older rocks to the north, beginning its 1,600-kilometre (1,000 mile) course just 65 kilometres (40 miles) from the Atlantic coast. For tiny Uruguay, it remains something to be proud of that, even in Brazil, the river retains its name—Uruguai—right to its source.

From the Second World War to Today

Some years ago a major tourist attraction drew people to the waterfront in Montevideo. It was the control tower of the German battleship, *Graf Spee,* which had been sunk in the River Plate during the Second World War. The Uruguayans did not actively take part in hostilities, but the incident of the *Graf Spee* served to indicate that the country's sympathies lay with the Allies in Europe.

In 1939, three British cruisers—*Exeter, Ajax and Achilles*—were despatched to the South Atlantic with orders to protect the transport routes over which vital food supplies were carried from the River Plate to Europe. The *Graf Spee* was sighted on December 13, and was hit in the ensuing battle. She was damaged and put into Montevideo harbour for repairs. The Uruguayan government, according to the terms of war, gave the *Graf Spee* four days before she must put out to sea again. The British cruisers waited outside the harbour. When the two sides met again in open water, the *Graf Spee* had little chance.

She was exploded and scuttled by her commander, and her crew made their way to Argentina, where they were welcomed as heroes.

During the war Argentina allied itself with the Axis powers, Germany and Italy, and applied pressure on Uruguay to do the same. But Uruguay, influenced as it had been for many years by the democratic principles of France, England and other parts of Europe, steadfastly refused to do so. Instead, it elected to allow the United States of America to establish air and naval bases in the country, and also accepted financial and technical assistance from the Americans.

By the end of the war, Uruguay's relations with Argentina were far from good. The most famous of Argentina's Presidents, General Peron, was in power and opponents to his regime fled to Montevideo, where they could work together plotting to overthrow the general. Uruguayan radio and newspapers were widely used for propaganda against him. By way of retaliation, Peron forbade Argentinians to travel to Uruguay, where they liked to take their holidays. His action had the desired disastrous effect on the Uruguayan economy, virtually closing down all the tourist trade. The situation only returned to normal after Peron was deposed in 1955 and the frontiers were reopened, much to the relief of the people of both countries.

Uruguay's wool and meat were in great demand during both world wars and during the Korean War in the 1950s, opening up a lucrative European market. At the same time, because of the difficulty of obtaining goods from Europe, there was a significant drop in the amount of consumer goods being imported into the country. As a consequence, small industries were begun which prospered, filling the gap created by the decline in imports. The standard of living improved. The market for consumer goods within the country grew bigger, the number of people without work declined. Educational opportunities opened up, working conditions were improved and better social security measures were introduced.

But things went badly wrong in the 1960s and 1970s, leading to social upheaval, strikes, economic crisis, and urban terrorism. These culminated in 1973 with the military taking over the government. Unlike almost every other country in South America, Uruguay had not been subject to military rule at any time in the twentieth century, and it came as a nasty shock to the people.

There were a number of reasons for this change in the country's fortunes. Firstly, the welfare state was proving too costly to maintain. Secondly, the constitutional argument never ceased from the time Batlle y Ordonez introduced the idea of a National Council of Administration. The debate over President versus the Council left the people confused and divided. Thirdly, Uruguay was dependent for its foreign currency on income earned from the export of beef and wool, and its economy was controlled by the world market price for these commodities. The world market price, which had remained high during wartime, dropped badly afterwards. And, finally, the production of beef and wool was badly affected by confused government plans to improve agricultural output, specifically in the production of wheat.

The government decided to make the republic self-sufficient in wheat, and accordingly offered farmers subsidies to encourage them to grow more. The subsidies proved to be so popular that this action led to a great deal of grazing land being converted to agriculture. Soon it was discovered that too much wheat was being produced. This over-production coincided with a time when world demand was falling, and the government had to sell the wheat at an uneconomic price. Storing the wheat was not practicable, as there were insufficient storage facilities, so the government and country suffered severe losses.

With some of the best land ploughed up for the wheat, there was less good pasture-land for the sheep and cattle, and the number of animals dropped. The meat-packing plants then found they could not obtain enough animals, and the export trade suffered accordingly. The situation was made worse because wool was fetching high world prices, and a number of farmers were persuaded to switch from cattle to sheep.

Many workers lost their jobs. Meat became expensive and hard to get; and, for the first time ever, Uruguayan housewives were faced with a "black market", which meant they were forced to pay very high prices for illegal supplies of meat.

The effect of this policy was a drop in export earnings, the dollars and sterling necessary to pay for imports and the purchase of new machinery and equipment. As the standard of living dropped, and people found they could no longer afford to buy

Slum housing in Montevideo. In recent years, Uruguay's once high standard of living has fallen dramatically, with many families experiencing great poverty and hardship

the goods they needed, they began to riot and demonstrate against the government.

Social discontent was not halted when, in 1958, elections were held and the ruling Colorado Party were defeated for the first time in ninety-three years. The Blancos promised an improvement in the economy which, in the event, they were unable to achieve. The resulting deterioration led to more strikes, riots, and demonstrations. A second term for the Blancos did nothing to improve the situation, and it was made worse by the emergence of urban guerrillas, whose widespread terrorist activities made newspaper headlines around the world.

The guerrillas took the name Tupamaros—from Tupac-

Amaru, the last of the Inca leaders in eighteenth-century Peru. One of the main weapons used by the Tupamaros to apply pressure on their own government, was to kidnap foreigners, sometimes to kill them.

The government's response was to declare a state of emergency. It set out to crush the Tupamaros. Thousands of people were detained without being accused of a crime, or being brought to trial. Censorship was imposed on the newspapers and television so that they could not write or say all they knew. And the trade unions were stopped from meeting and demonstrating.

No one was surprised when, in 1973, the armed forces intervened. Over night they took control of the government, and Congress was closed. They used repressive measures which were not at all welcome to a people with a democratic tradition and they are alleged to have had more political prisoners per head of population than any other country in the world. Despite borrowing huge amounts of money from international banks and other countries, the generals were not able to improve the economy. The once high standard of living declined even further. The shortage of food and the increased prices led to widespread malnutrition, particularly among old people and children.

The military rulers were extremely unpopular, because of their attitude towards people who did not agree with them, and also because of their failure to improve the economy. The people began to demand a return to democracy. The military rulers

Posters calling for the release of political prisoners during the elections held in November 1984

were prepared to agree to a partial return to democracy but they wanted to retain control over some aspects of government. A compromise was reached whereby elections for a new President would go ahead, but, within months of his taking office, in March 1985, an agreement would be reached to decide on the role of the armed forces in the future government.

Many people were unhappy to accept this compromise. Nonetheless, the political parties, the Reds and Whites, (Colorados and Blancos), and a number of smaller parties, agreed to proceed. The period before these elections, however, was overshadowed by the "Ferreira affair". Ferreira, leader of the Whites and one of Uruguay's most popular politicians, returned to his homeland after many years in exile. So nervous were the military that they sent no less than five warships and supporting aircraft to intercept the ferry on which Ferreira was travelling. Although threatened with arrest, Ferreira determined to proceed to Uruguay, and he was detained immediately upon his arrival there. He had been the favourite to win the presidency; now the elections were to go ahead without him.

Señor Sanguinetti, the leader of the Colorado Party won the election and was sworn in as President on March 1, 1985. Congress was also reopened, and changes in the constitution are promised. The armed forces left the political scene, but not without a warning that, if it proved necessary, they would once again take control.

Much now depends on the ability of the new government to

"Long live democracy"—a banner displayed during the 1984 elections. Uruguay has now returned to democratic government, but the country's problems are not yet over

manage the economy, and meet the demands of the people for an improved standard of living. This promises to be a difficult task, but the first essential rung of the ladder—the return to democratic government—has now been achieved.

Index